Animals and Human Culture

Contents

What to Do

1.
Predict

Say to your group:
"I predict that this page is going to be about..."

You can use these things to help you predict:

- photographs
- captions
- headings
- what you already know.

Now all of the group should read the page silently.

2.
Clarify

When you have all finished reading, find out if the group need to clarify the meaning of anything they have read or any particular vocabulary.

Say: *"Is there anything we need to clarify?"*

Encourage your group to:

- use a dictionary to look up unknown words
- compare definitions in two or three dictionaries and a thesaurus to find the best meaning for the word in the text
- look up places in an atlas.

After your research say: *"Does anyone have anything to add to that?"*

Now:

- choose a face
- when you see your face, you are the leader
- when you are the leader, it's your job to get everyone talking about the page.

3.
Ask Questions

Lead your group in a discussion about what they have read.
Say: *"Does anyone have a question they would like to put to the group?"*

Encourage your group to talk about what they have found interesting or puzzling. Challenge them to create questions about the text.
You could ask: who..., what..., where..., when..., why..., how... or what if...

If there is a stop sign on your page, ask the question and encourage everyone in the group to say something.

4.
Summarise

After discussion, outline the main points of what you have read. Remember to refer to comments from other members of the group and things that you have looked up.
Say: *"My summary of what we have read is..."*

Early People and Animals

Human beings are involved with many animal communities on Earth. People may hunt some animals, they could be the master or friend of others, and they are even prey to others. In fact, some scientists believe that early humans were more likely to be prey than predators. The animal predators that lived alongside early humans thousands and thousands of years ago were much larger than their descendants that live today, and they greatly outnumbered the humans.

As early people became more skilled as hunters, however, they found ways to hunt animals that were larger, stronger and swifter than them. Early people made up for their lack of strength against these animals by using weapons and by hunting in groups. By doing this they could ambush their prey, encircle it, trap it in pits or chase it over cliffs.

Then, about 10,000 to 12,000 years ago, people began domesticating animals, and became less dependent on hunting as a main food source. Still, people continued to hunt animals. People have also kept animals as pets, and in circuses and zoos.

Today, many people still hunt animals, sometimes just for sport. However, many countries now have laws that protect animals against pain and suffering. These countries recognise the right of all animals to live freely on our Earth.

A 3D model of prehistoric hunters trapping an ancient animal in a bog

Does anyone have a question they would like to put to the group?

My summary of what we have read is...

Respect for an Ancient Animal

I predict that this page is going to be about…

People have long been both curious about and fearful of animals. They have shown animals great respect and given them special treatment, even while hunting and killing them for food.

As early as one hundred thousand years ago, at a place called Drachenloch in the Swiss Alps, there is some evidence that Neanderthal hunters placed a number of cave bear skulls in stone chests and buried them deep inside a dwelling. Nobody knows for sure why they might have done this, but some people think it could have been out of respect for the cave bear. Prehistoric cave bears were similar to grizzly bears, only bigger. They would have been a fearsome sight, with their razor-sharp claws and huge teeth. When they reared up on their hind feet, they stood about three metres tall. The hunters, who were armed only with stone weapons, would have feared them.

Cave bears have been extinct for thousands of years. While no one knows for sure why they died out, it is certain that the bears competed with early humans for food and shelter. Perhaps people's ability to plan and hunt creatively gave them an edge in survival that allowed them to live, while the bears died out.

STOP

When you read, "a fearsome sight," what picture do you get in your head?

Is there anything we need to clarify?

A large adult grizzly bear can rear up to a height of nearly two metres on its hind legs – a little taller than an average adult person, and a scary sight. Yet imagine a prehistoric cave bear doing the same thing. Although similar in appearance, the cave bear would have towered to an impressive three metres in height.

3 m

2 m

A roaring grizzly bear

Does anyone have a question they would like to put to the group?

My summary of what we have read is...

Animals in Cave Paintings

In the caves that sheltered early people from the bitter weather of the last great ice age, anthropologists have discovered other evidence of human interest in animals. The walls of limestone caves in France and Spain are covered with thousands of paintings, mostly of animals. Many of these paintings show animals trapped, wounded or dying. No one knows for sure why these early artists showed so many of the animals wounded or, in fact, why they painted them at all. Some experts believe that people created the paintings to bring the hunter good luck. It is also possible that they created the paintings to record a memorable hunt.

Anthropologists know that the Cro-Magnon people who created these paintings did not have an easy time. They had to crawl on their stomachs, through mazes of narrow tunnels, into the deep, dark, secret places in the caves. The question is, why did they do this? So, scientists study modern hunter-gatherers to learn more. Were the people painting their dreams? Were they painting their past? While no one knows for sure, it is certain that animals played an important part in the people's lives.

STOP

When you read, "mazes of narrow tunnels," what picture do you get in your head?

Is there anything we need to clarify?

8

Animals are the main subject in cave paintings around the world.

A 3D model of Cro-Magnon people painting deep in a cave

Does anyone have a question they would like to put to the group?

My summary of what we have read is...

Animals and Ancient Egyptians

Animal Qualities Admired

Since early times, people have admired animals for their qualities. The ancient Egyptians believed that certain animals were equal or superior to humans, usually because they feared and respected the animals for their power. People learned to live alongside dangerous creatures such as crocodiles, snakes and scorpions. While they understood the animals' threat, they also admired the characteristics that made the animals powerful.

The crocodile was probably the most feared and respected animal. Its strength, speed and skill as a hunter were qualities the ancient Egyptians believed were necessary in their ruler, the pharaoh. Some crocodiles, after their death, were mummified and buried in sacred coffins.

The ancient Egyptians also worshipped the cobra, even though this deadly creature terrified them. The shape of it reared up in defence became a symbol of protection. The cobra was on many Egyptian shrines, and the pharaoh wore a double crown with an upright form of this spitting snake.

Many other animals were sacred to the ancient Egyptians. The small venomous scorpion, greatly feared by the ancient Egyptians, was believed to protect the goddess Isis from her enemies.

I predict that this page is going to be about...

Is there anything we need to clarify?

This painted wall shows the cobra as a symbol on the pharaoh's crown as well as on the crown of Isis.

Early Egyptians worshipped hundreds of gods, and many were shown as animals or as human figures with animal heads such as Sobek, the crocodile god.

Does anyone have a question they would like to put to the group?

My summary of what we have read is...

Animals Mummified

I predict that this page is going to be about…

The bodies of pets and sacred Egyptian animals were often mummified, and their mummified bodies have been found in tombs. The ancient Egyptians loved their pets, so they carefully preserved them for a long life after death. The animals were prepared for burial like humans, then carefully wrapped and either buried in a tomb of their own, or alongside a person.

One of the most common animal mummies in ancient Egypt was the cat. The cat was an extremely important part of Egyptian life. Ancient Egyptians thought that it represented the goddess Bastet, who was often shown as a woman with the head of a desert cat. Cats were sacred to Bastet and to harm one was often punishable by death. Many cats were raised in the temples, and when they died they were mummified and buried in huge cemeteries. Some sacred animals were considered so important to the Egyptians that they were given a royal burial.

In later Egyptian times, people raised animals specifically to turn into mummies. These mummies were sold to people who were on their way to a temple to worship a god. The people would leave the mummified animals there as an offering.

The ancient Egyptians had a very close relationship with the animal world and almost every kind of animal that lived in those days has been found as a mummy.

The goddess Bastet's symbol, the cat, was held in high regard.

Is there anything we need to clarify?

A mummified cat and a cat sarcophagus

STOP

OPINION

Do you think animals should have been given burials like a pharaoh's? Why? Why not?

Other animals important to Egyptian life, such as the crocodile, were also mummified.

Does anyone have a question they would like to put to the group?

My summary of what we have read is...

Animals as Symbols

In many cultures throughout the world, animals hold incredible power and people use many of them as symbols.

Some people have myths that feature powerful animals creating the world. In Australia, the Aboriginal people tell a story about a huge python, known as the rainbow serpent, that writhed over the land, and created all of the mountains, rivers, valleys, lakes and large, flat places.

Many Native American cultures believe that, from birth, a person has a special connection with a certain animal and that most of these animals have symbols attached to them. The bear, for example, can be a symbol of power, patience, gentleness, strength and dreaming, while the ant might be a symbol of teamwork.

In Chinese culture, animal symbols are everywhere. Statues of animals appear throughout China as signs of wealth and good luck. The mythical dragon is a very important part of the culture and a powerful symbol of good fortune. For Chinese people, the dragon symbolises justice, peace and harmony. When it is shared with other cultures, it is a symbol of protection and support for all.

The characteristics of animals can mean different things to different cultures. To some Native Americans the wolf is a symbol of loyalty, while many European cultures consider the wolf a frightening animal.

In the Chinese New Year the dragon is used to symbolise happiness and good fortune and is paraded through the streets.

Some Native American cultures use animals such as the wolf to symbolise certain human traits. BELOW: An Arapaho man wears a wolf's head to a pow wow or meeting.

Does anyone have a question they would like to put to the group?

My summary of what we have read is...

Animals in Fiction

I predict that this page is going to be about...

Throughout human history, animals have been the subject of stories. In the sixth century BC, legend has it that a Greek slave named Aesop travelled to many places after he became a free man, collecting stories as he went. These were oral tales handed down from generation to generation. These stories gave animals human qualities and each one had a moral message.

Many other authors have used animals to show human characteristics and give a message that was really about human behaviour. There are different ways animals can be used to do this. Sometimes they are portrayed as humans. Sometimes they are animals interacting with humans, and sometimes they are portrayed as animals interacting only with other animals.

In the story of *Charlotte's Web*, author EB White used talking animals to communicate the messages of friendship, affection, protection, selfishness, trust and betrayal. There is a selfish rat and a lovable pig, who is saved by an intelligent spider. Throughout the story these characters act and talk like humans. They don't interact with humans but they act in ways that humans would.

Wilbur heaved himself down in an agony of pain and sorrow. Great sobs racked his body. He heaved and grunted with desolation. "Charlotte," he moaned. "Charlotte, my true friend."

Is there anything we need to clarify?

STOP

What connections can you make with stories you have read in which animals acted like humans?

Does anyone have a question they would like to put to the group?

Two early stories showing animals with human qualities: Aesop's fable, "The Wolf and the Crane", and a Prussian tale about a fox and a cat.

My summary of what we have read is...

The Domestication of Animals

I predict that this page is going to be about...

The domestication of animals began more than 10,000 years ago, while Stone Age people were still nomadic hunters. Among the animals they hunted were wolves, which, like them, travelled in family groups. Wolves were scavengers and competed with the humans for the same prey. Sometimes, hunters would kill mother wolves but spare the cubs. The cubs were friendly, easily tamed and useful as decoys. Eventually, the wolf cubs evolved into domesticated dogs.

Towards the end of the last ice age, people became more successful at cultivating grains and this led to the beginnings of human settlement. They continued domesticating animals. People may have first separated sheep and goats from their wild herds, and then kept them and killed them when needed for food. Domestication is a slow process. The most successfully domesticated animals are those whose ancestors lived in family groups, packs or herds.

People domesticated animals for different reasons: for food, products to sell or trade, work, transportation or to keep as pets. An animal is considered domesticated when it has new traits that are not found in the wild, it is kept for a reason, its breeding is controlled and its survival depends on humans.

STOP
OPINION
Do you think people should have domesticated animals? Why? Why not?

Is there anything we need to clarify?

Egyptian fresco, from about 1300BC, shows oxen being used to plow fields.

Cave painting of domesticated cattle from about 4000BC

Domestication and controlled breeding of animals has resulted in a variety of different characteristics that no longer resemble their ancestors'.

Does anyone have a question they would like to put to the group?

My summary of what we have read is...

Breeding Animals

Over the years, people have bred animals to do special tasks. A good example is the difference between the cat and the dog.

All domesticated cats probably descended from African wild cats, which were solitary animals. Although cats have lost much of the wildness of their ancestors, they remain solitary and aloof. Cats are not pack animals that depend on a group leader, so they are not likely to work for people.

Dogs, however, descended from the wolf. They are sociable and dependent on people, and are much more interested in being part of a group. The earliest dogs probably were like Australian dingoes, which are descendants of the dogs that people carried over from Asia about 8000 years ago. Many dogs today do not look much like their wolf ancestors, although they are the same species. This is because dogs have been bred for different purposes – hunting, working, guarding and, of course, companionship.

Humans have carefully bred animals to provide a product such as meat or skins. However, other animals, such as elephants, have not been changed by humans. It takes so long for an elephant to grow to maturity that it would cost too much to breed them.

I predict that this page is going to be about...

Is there anything we need to clarify?

What are the similarities and differences between the animals?

Animals for Entertainment

Since ancient times, people have kept animals in captivity and used them for entertainment. In Egypt and China, rulers often kept their own animal menageries.

These menageries often featured unusual animals that came from faraway lands. Travellers would tell stories of the rare animals they'd seen, and the rulers collected these animals to prove how wealthy and powerful they were. They would then allow other people to come and view the fascinating creatures. At one point in his reign, a Roman emperor named Octavius Augustus kept 420 tigers, 260 lions, 600 African cheetahs and leopards, a rhinoceros, a hippopotamus – and more.

Today, however, people have different opinions about keeping animals for entertainment. Some people think it is cruel to force animals to perform tricks and behave in a way that no creature would behave in the wild, and that people should never keep these animals in captivity for any reason. Others believe that zoos play an important role in helping to protect some endangered species, saving them from extinction.

Throughout the ages, people have tested their intelligence and skill against the superior physical powers of animals for sport. A surviving example today is bullfighting. Like circuses and zoos, many people believe bullfighting is cruel, while others think it is an important part of Spanish culture.

I predict that this page is going to be about...

A nine-year-old matador fights a young bull.

An elephant performs for its trainer at the Bouglione Circus in Paris.

Is there anything we need to clarify?

Animals in Medicine

I predict that this page is going to be about...

Throughout history, animals have played an important part in medicine. Since the Middle Ages, people have used leeches in bloodletting, a procedure they believed necessary to cure many common illnesses, and they used maggots to clean wounds. Some Indian tribes in South America still use the mandibles from soldier ants as clips to close wounds.

Almost every important medical discovery has happened using animals for research. In 1922, two Canadian researchers found that a dog suffered from diabetes when its pancreas was removed. Insulin, a hormone that a person with diabetes needs, is now made in a laboratory, but it was originally taken from dog pancreases. Scientists also used dogs in research that led to the development of modern anaesthetics, and still use hamsters and mice in cancer research.

An AIDS researcher handling mice that have been given a human immune system

There are so many ways that animals have helped with medical research: kidney transplants, polio vaccines, heart-valve replacements and life-support systems for premature babies. However, there is much debate about whether people need to use animals in this way. Some scientists think that if animals weren't used in medical research, then advances would slow down. Other people think that it is immoral to use animals this way and that scientists can achieve the same results without using them.

STOP

What can you infer about the mandibles of soldier ants?

Is there anything we need to clarify?

In this 16th-century painting, a doctor uses a leech to extract contaminated blood in the Leeches Chamber.

At the Westchester Medical Centre in New York, leeches are used after reconstructive surgery.

Does anyone have a question they would like to put to the group?

My summary of what we have read is...

Since early times, people have coexisted in many different ways and in the same environments as animals. Even though they have preyed on each other, there has still been a very important relationship between them. While animals provide food, help with medical research, and even entertainment, they are, most importantly, the objects of love and affection.

Some people see their pets as teachers and healers. For many generations, Native Americans recognised that animals could teach them many things. Dogs demonstrated loyalty, cats independence and horses strength. Today, animals can provide therapy for patients in hospitals, act as guides for people with disabilities, assist the police in finding and detaining criminals, or help in rescues.

It is important to understand the great contribution that animals make to our lives. Sadly, at times we have taken animals for granted, and used and dominated them. People's actions have often shown a lack of respect for these living beings.

Of all the animal species, are people the ones who truly need to learn how to share our world with others?

I predict that this page is going to be about...

A guide dog with its owner

An avalanche rescue dog

Is there anything we need to clarify?

Here, a donkey is used as part of an animal pet therapy programme run in retirement homes.

Does anyone have a question they would like to put to the group?

My summary of what we have read is...

Something to Think About

DEBATABLE STATEMENT

Animals should not be used for entertainment.

AGAINST

?

FOR

?

MIDDLE POSITION

?

CONCLUSION

?

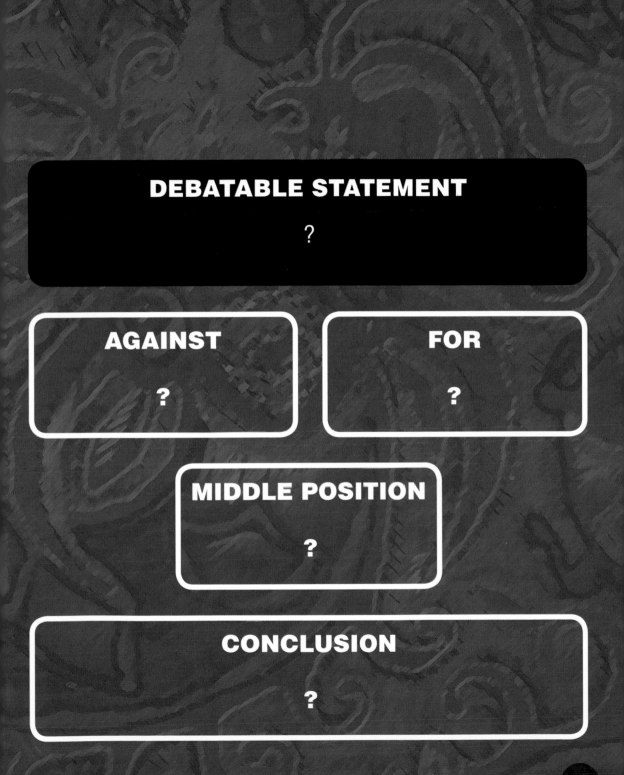

DEBATABLE STATEMENT

?

AGAINST

?

FOR

?

MIDDLE POSITION

?

CONCLUSION

?

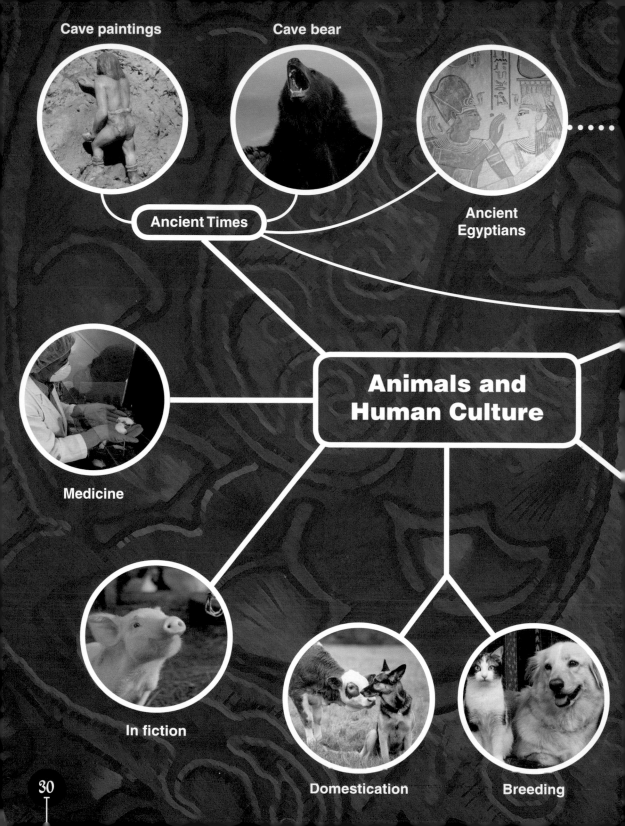

Cave paintings

Cave bear

Ancient Egyptians

Ancient Times

Animals and Human Culture

Medicine

In fiction

Domestication

Breeding

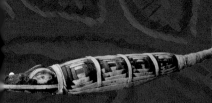
Mummified animals

Symbols

Entertainment

Review

Once you have finished reading the book, draw together the thoughts and findings of your group. You may find the following sentence starters useful:

We learned...
We thought...
We questioned...
We wondered...
We discussed...
We argued about...
We were amazed by...
We were puzzled by...
We weren't sure about...
We want to know more about...
Three things we remember are...

Index